A BRIEF HISTORY OF FINLAND

OTAVA PUBLISHING COMPANY LTD.
HELSINKI

A Brief History of Finland

Matti Klinge

Photographs: Department of Museums pp. 30, 44, 47, 60, 64, 70—71, 81; Finnish Air Force picture archives pp. 38—39; Finnish Architectural Museum pp. 14, 89, 155; Helsinki City Museum, pp. 54—55; Seppo Hilpo p. 114; Lehtikuva pp. 12, 120, 134, 140, 144, 145, 148, 149 (upper), 151, 152; Otava picture archives pp. 20—21, 24, 26, 31, 32—33, 46, 52, 56, 58—59, 62, 66, 68—69, 82—83, 88, 92—93, 94—95, 99, 123; Pressfoto pp. 107, 132, 137, 142, 149 (below), 157, 158; Istvan Racz p. 8; Fred Runeberg p. 79; Esa Santakari p. 42; Suomen taideteollisuusyhdistys p. 138; Vuokko p. 139; Wärtsilä p. 130; Yhtyneitten kuva-arkisto pp. 11, 117, 124, 127, 148.

4th, revised edition 1987

Translated by *David Mitchell*
Designed by *Markku Reunanen*

Kustannusosakeyhtiö Otavan painolaitokset
Keuruu 1987

Printed in Finland

ISBN 951-1-09451-3

Contents

Finland before 1155 7

The Era of the Crusades 10

Part of the Kingdom of Sweden 17

    The Birth of the Centralized State 25

    The Great Power 35

    Russian Expansion Westwards in the 18th
    Century 41

The Autonomous Grand Duchy 50

Independent Finland 97

Finland before 1155

Some ten thousand years ago, following the retreat of the continental ice-sheet, the first scattered settlements began to appear on the broad expanse of land, covered with lakes and forests, between the Gulf of Finland, the Gulf of Bothnia and Lake Ladoga. It is thought that the inhabitants of this area belonged racially and linguistically to the Finno-Ugrian group of peoples long before the Finns who gave their name to the country and its people migrated from the southern reaches of the Gulf of Finland to the south-western part of the Finnish peninsula at the beginning of the Christian calendar. But there is a difference, thousands of years old, between the inland and coastal areas of this region; it is reflected in the way of life of the people and in their artifacts and is probably based on different racial and cultural traditions. Western influences, particularly from Scandinavia but also from south of the Baltic Sea, have played a central part in Finland's pre-history and in the making of the modern nation. Recent research into the hereditary nature of blood groups indicates that about three-quarters of the present Finnish nation is of western racial origin and one-third of eastern; the western element is strongest in the west of the country and along the coast. On the other

An elkhead club from Huittinen in south-west Finland — about 5000 years old. Animal-head weapons of this sort, carved from soapstone, have been found in many parts of the country and far to the east.

hand, the linguistic structure of the modern nation shows that the eastern language has been stronger than the western and that a great many inhabitants of Germanic origin have adopted the various dialects of Finnish, with the apparent exception of the very latest arrivals from the west and their offspring. But a number of factors which were not present during earlier periods of migration and cultural dissemination now helped the language of these latest arrivals to survive.

The Viking expeditions, of which there are written records since about the year 800, made their way not only west from Scandinavia but also to the east. The eastern route went through the Lake Mälaren valley and the Götaland region, onward through the Gulf of Finland under the shelter of the Finnish archipelago to Lake Ladoga and from there, southwards along the waterways, as far as Constantinople. The Vikings ruled in Novgorod in 862, in Kiev in 882 and, as early as 860, they had made their first attack on the capital of the eastern Roman Empire. According to runic stones many Swedes were still making journeys to Russia and Byzantium in the 10th and 11th centuries, some of them settling there. Inhabitants of the area now known as Finland certainly took part in these expeditions. On the other hand, a south-north sea system linked what now is southern and eastern Finland to the south coast of the Baltic, Pomerania and Prussia, and to the eastern coast, Livonia and Estonia. Different cultural, religious, economic and conceptual influences came to Finland in this way from Central Europe, until the German, Danish and Swedish expansions westwards at the beginning of the 13th century put a definite stop to this system. The Finnish national epic Kalevala depicts in its heroic songs reminiscences from this period of "the Baltic Vikings".

The Era of the Crusades

At the dawn of the historical era the area that later became Finland was not yet a united whole. The main tribes, the Finns proper, the Tavastians and the Karelians differed from each other in many respects and were often hostile to each other. The Finns had connections to the west and south, the Karelians to the south-east; furthermore, the Åland Islands and part of Western Finland and the archipelago had belonged since an earlier period to the Central Swedish military and economic system. In the 11th century expeditions were made from Sweden and Denmark to western Finland. They followed the old eastern route of the Vikings and were evidently also undertaken in competition with Novgorod. The Kingdom of Sweden, now coming into being with the Uppsala-Sigtuna district at its centre, sought to stabilize old economic and cultural links with western Finland.

Tradition has it that the first crusade, led by King Eric and St. Henry, the Bishop of Uppsala, was undertaken to extend the area of the Swedish influence. Missionary work was conducted on the one hand, towards the old central area of Turku, and on the other, towards the inner regions the country, around the present city of Tampere.

The fact that St. Henry was of English origin links the establishment of the Finnish missionary diocese with the general development in Scandinavia. The Catholic Church came to Finland from England after attempts to introduce it from northern Germany had failed. Although there are virtually no written sources describing Finnish history in the 12th century, the scant historical evidence that does exist, together with more plentiful archaelogical findings, is sufficient to show that Christianity took permanent root in south-western Finland and that religious, economic and political links developed between this area and Svealand and east Götaland. At the same time Novgorod was taking an open interest in the people and trading places along the shores of the Gulf of Finland and Lake Ladoga. This area too was united by religious, economic and political interests.

The Danes and Germans were also interested in the coastal regions along the old eastern route. Sweden failed in its attempt to gain influence in western Estonia and it was the King

of Denmark who conquered the western and northern parts of the country and established Tallin in 1219. At the same time the Teutonic Knights were attempting to push northwards and gained temporary hold of Estonia but it was soon re-taken by the Danes. Meanwhile the second crusade, from Sweden into Tavastia, had taken place under the leadership of Earl Birger. With Sweden in control of Tavastia and the establishment of a castle there, the coast of eastern Uusimaa (Nyland) began to be settled by groups of Swedish immigrants. The centre of the area was probably Porvoo (Borgå). The aim behind these measures was to provide support for attempts at expansion towards the east. While the Mongolians attacked Russia from the east, the Swedish "Prince" and his troops, whose numbers included bishops as well as Finns and Tavastians, pushed their way as far as the River Neva. It was here in 1240 that they were defeated by Alexander Nevski, the Prince of Novgorod, who two years later defeated the Germans in Estonia.

In the 13th century a loosely defined border dividing Swedish and Novgorod interests took shape. It extended from the River Kymi

Turku Castle, Finland's oldest medieval castle. Building was begun on it in the 13th century and it was completed at the end of the 16th century. It was here that John, Duke of Finland, and his wife Catherine Jagellonica held court in Renaissance style in the 1560's.

through eastern Tavastia to a point somewhere on the coast of the Gulf of Bothnia. The decisive struggle for possession of the eastern coast of the Gulf of Finland and inland Finland was fought at the end of the 13th and beginning of the 14th centuries. In 1293 Sweden embarked on the third crusade and founded the Wiborg fortress and city. During an expedition undertaken in 1300, the Swedes founded the Landskrona fortress on the banks of the River Neva, but this was destroyed by Novgorod. The long period of war came to an end with the Treaty of Pähkinäsaari (Schlüsselburg now Petrokrepost) in 1323. It was here that, for the first time, the border between Sweden and Novgorod (later Russia) was agreed; not only a political border, it was also to divide two religions and two cultures. The people of Savo and western Karelia, whom destiny had placed to the west of the border were to grow up, alongside the Tavastians and Finns, within the political and cultural sphere of the Kingdom of Sweden and under the Roman Catholic Church. The Swedish settlements in Uusimaa and along the coastal areas of Karelia, the

The interior of the Church of the Holy Cross at Hattula: the paintings in this 13th century brick-church were executed in the 16th century before the onset of the Reformation. In the foreground, dating from about 1560, is one of the oldest Lutheran pulpits in Finland. The church was a well known place of pilgrimage throughout Catholic Scandinavia.

Wiborg and later the Olavinlinna fortresses, as well as the influence of trade and traders tied this area and its inhabitants to the West. Similarly, the Karelians, whom fate had placed east of the border, formed ever closer ties with Novgorod and the Orthodox Church. Later, the areas of North Karelia, Käkisalmi and the Karelian Isthmus were to be annexed to the Kingdom of Sweden and later still to the Finnish Grand Duchy. Thus the area, the people and the traditions that comprise modern Finland embrace Orthodox elements from east of the border as it was in the Middle Ages. However, the Finnish peninsula and its inhabitants were essentially linked to the emerging Swedish state and the Catholic Church. Indeed, the Karelians long referred to their western tribal brothers as "Swedes", a fact which demonstrates that, along the centuries, administrative and religious factors proved to be stronger than a common ancestry in the shaping of a nation's culture. The Finnish tribes, then, differed decisively from the Karelians and Estonians and joined the tribes of Sweden and the state growing up around them.

Part of the Kingdom of Sweden

In the Middle Ages, as part of the Kingdom of Sweden, Finland had no special status which might have been reflected in such things as a separate administration, different laws or an addition to the King's title. From the outset the Kingdom was essentially a community which had grown up around the sea and the waterways (Lake Mälare) leading to the sea. The sea was to remain the most important means of transport and communication until the era of the railways. Cultural, commercial and administrative development in the peasant Kingdom of Sweden and in the areas to the east and west of the sea were largely dependent on influences from further south. From the beginning of the 13th century onwards the country experienced a change of decisive importance when the early influence of the English Church was replaced by a German merchant and city-centred culture. At the same time members of the nobility from the south coast of the Baltic and even further afield moved into the country mostly to fill military and legal positions. Estonia, the whole of which had come under the control of the Teutonic Knights in 1346 and whose capital had been predominantly German for some time, exerted a powerful influence throughout the Gulf of

Finland area, as far as Turku and Stockholm. The influence of Sweden in the Middle Ages, on the other hand, can be seen clearly from the fact that only rarely did the families of the old local chieftains rise to the ranks of the nobility which had developed along with the system of castles and castle administration. On the other hand, the Swedish peasant settlements in Uusimaa and Ostrobothnia grew up, side by side, with the Finnish, creating a unified western Finnish culture despite the maintenance of two seperate languages. This culture can be said, perhaps, to have resembled that of eastern Sweden (Uppland — East Götaland) more than that of eastern Finland from which it differed in respect to traditions in agriculture, the family, artifacts and food.

An important feature of development in the 14th and 15th centuries was the way the Bishop's Seat in Turku, and the entire Church organization, established its position and thrived both spiritually and materially. As the ecclesiastical culture spread and took deeper root it tied Finland to the general sphere of European Christian culture. Gradually, stone churches, decorated with carvings and paintings, were built in all parts of inhabited Finland. The arrival in Finland of various monastic orders, including Dominicans, Franciscans, indigent orders and, later, the Order of St. Bridget, which took their place alongside the regular congregational clergy, strengthened the power of the Church. Journeys to the Papal curia in Avignon or Rome and, in particular, study trips to the famous universities on the continent, all of which formed part of the universal ecclesiastical culture of the Middle Ages, further advanced Finland's spiritual integration with Europe. Together with urban culture the influence of the church was felt specifically in the relatively densely populated areas of western Finland and was naturally weaker in those areas where, in addition to agriculture, life still revolved to a large extent round hunting trips and other forms of livelihood requiring mobility. The most important centres from which the new influences spread were Turku, with its Bishop's seat and Cathedral, and Wiborg, both of which were the home of a number of important figures of medieval bourgeois society, particularly members of the artisan professions. The people of these towns had close contacts with the bourgeois culture of Tallin, Stockholm, Danzig and Lübeck, a culture which in the Middle Ages was largely German orientated.

At the centre of the Kingdom the name Eastland was sometimes applied to Finland (Proper) and the other areas beyond the sea, evidently in the same way that Northland began to be used as a general name for the provinces to the north of the centre. Eastland and Northland formed important and organic links with the centre formed around Svealand

The Kuitia Manor at Parainen (c. 1490—1540), a well-preserved residential manor, built by Joakim and Erik Fleming.

and Götaland. In the 1350's and once more in the 1440's a common Law of the Land was drawn up. It was compiled on the basis of the old provincial laws. Such laws had been unknown in Finland and Northland. In about 1350 a general Town Law was also drawn up. Thus Swedish law and a Scandinavian social system became established in Finland. They were to remain permanent national characteristics, features which distinguish the culture of the Finns from that of the Karelians and the Estonians. The right of representatives of the Finnish body of *lagman* (law-man = the country's highest magistrate) to participate in the election of the King was confirmed in 1362. This legal system, together with the four-estate representation (the nobility, the clergy, the burghers and the farmers) which had developed since the beginning of the 15th century, gave Finland indisputable and full political rights within the Kingdom of Sweden – unlike those countries which were defeated and annexed to the Kingdom later in the 16th and 17th centuries.

During the period of the Scandinavian (Kalmar) Union in the 15th and beginning of the 16th centuries, the influence of Denmark was felt in Finland too. Supporters of the Union and those opposed to it (they might better be described as opponents to each successive leader of the Union) met in open conflict, e.g. in the 1430's, the time of Engelbrekt

Engelbrektsson and the 1470's, the period of Sten Sture the elder. Finland cannot be said to have formed a political entity or unit where this issue was concerned, but in practice it did function as an area of economic support, securing power for Sten Sture for example. If it is possible to talk of nationalistic feelings at that time, in Finland too they were directed against the Danes.

The Pähkinäsaari Treaty of 1323 did not put an end to the question of the Swedish Kingdom's eastern border. Its southern reaches, it is true, were clearly defined and placed the districts of Jääski and Äyräpää on the Karelian Isthmus in Swedish territory, but the third area mentioned by name in the Treaty, Savo, because of the nature of its settlements and the forms of livelihood practiced there, was not nearly so well defined. A semi-nomadic way of life and slash-and-burn agriculture, which meant the constant clearing of new land for cultivation, led to a complex system of ownership and property rights. The border, which ran north from the Karelian Isthmus to the sea (the Gulf of Bothnia or perhaps the Arctic), was probably not in fact a border in the strict sense of the word, a situation which caused conflicts as communities began to expand. The Savo settlements spread out towards the east and, in the mid 1470's, the Lord of the Wiborg fortress, Erik Axelson Tott, built the Olavinlinna fortress on the border to

The frontispiece of the Missale Aboense, the missal of the Turku diocese – printed in Lübeck in 1488. In the centre is St. Henry the apostle of Finland and patron saint of Turku Cathedral, with the peasant Lalli, his assassin, at his feet. On their knees at either side of the Saint are the bishop, Konrad Bitz and Mauno Särkilahti, Dean of the Cathedral, with their coats of arms.

provide support for expansion. The influence of Karelia-Novgorod was gradually pushed back from the coast of the Gulf of Bothnia. At all events, the districts of Pohjanmaa (Ostrobothnia) and Länsipohja (Westrobothnia) were deemed part of the Kingdom of Sweden in 1346 when the border between the Uppsala and Turku diocese was fixed as running between the River Kemi and the River Kaakama. Thus, by virtue of its expanding settlements, Sweden gained considerable areas to the east of the border as it was defined in the Treaty of Pähkinäsaari, a fact which led to continuous border conflicts. Sweden ignored the continuous demands of Novgorod that it should mark out its border in the terrain. When the border was eventually re-drawn at the Peace Treaty of Täyssinä (1595), it more or less followed the eastern limits to the Savo settlements, a border which had in fact been established in practice much earlier and which, by continuing to the Arctic Sea, also confirmed Swedish (and Danish) supremacy in Lapland.

The Birth of the Centralized State

The collapse of the Scandinavian Union and the reign of Gustavus I Vasa (1523–1560) represented an important turning point in the history of the Swedish state and especially of its eastern territories.

Separation from Denmark and Norway on the one hand, and the Reformation, with its financial exploitation of the Church, on the other, led to Sweden's cultural isolation from the rest of Europe, with which it had become united in the international atmosphere of the 15th century. The trend to a more provincial culture, following the general principles of the Reformation, meant the appearance in Sweden of literature in both languages of the state, with the Bible translated into Swedish and (most of

ARMA MAGNI
DVCATVS
FiNLANDIÆ

it) into Finnish. Other ecclesiastical and legal works also appeared in both languages. In translating such works into Finnish, Michael Agricola, rector of the Cathedral school in Turku, who had studied under Luther and Melanchton at Wittenberg and would eventually become Bishop of Turku, laid the basis for a Finnish literature. Following the Reformation, with Gustavus Vasa's expropriation of church property, there was little support for advances in the field of culture. The state profited considerably from

---

Based on a Flemish model, this Renaissance coat of arms on Gustavus Vasa's tombstone in Upsala Cathedral is the prototype for the Finnish coat of arms.

A figure representing the ancient God Ilmarinen from the shaman's drum of the hundred-year-old Lapp, Andreas Poulsen who, in 1682 was accused of witchcraft. Particularly in the outlying areas of Lapland and Karelia it was still possible in the 20th century to record the ancient folk traditions of the Finns and the peoples related to them.

the "nationalization" of the Church. In the Kingdom now separated from Denmark, Finland held a position of real importance, a fact reflected in the role played by members of the Finnish nobility in state administration and the army in the 16th century.

During the reign of Gustavus Vasa the country's economic structure underwent a decisive change with taxation and financial administration, previously based on a system of castle *fiefs,* now the direct responsibility of the centralized state. The financial difficulties of the Crown, which led to the almost complete confiscation of Church property, was also behind the proclamation of 1542 claiming the uninhabited wilds of Finland as Crown property. This paved the way for extensive state-controlled territorial expansion, particularly in Savo where settlements built around the method of slash-and-burn agriculture spread hundreds of kilometres to the north and north-west.

Throughout the 16th century, right up until the Peace Treaty of Stolbova in 1617, Sweden's political relations with Russia played a central part in the country's affairs. Behind this was not only dissatisfaction with the border as it was defined at Pähkinäsaari but also changes within Russia, the Baltic and Poland. The war with Russia (1555−57) ended with neither side having achieved a clear victory. With the collapse of the Teutonic Knights in 1561, Tallin allied itself with Sweden, but throughout the 1570's fierce battles were fought with Russia both in Estonia and in Finland. Swedish victories between 1580 and 1581, particularly those at Käkisalmi and Narva, led to the addition of "Grand Duke of Finland, Karelia, Ingria and a fifth part of Vatja (Käkisalmi)" to King John III's title. These successes were due in part to the fact that Russia was being harassed by Poland at the same time.

With his marriage to Catherine Jagellonica in 1563, John III had already strengthened Sweden's ties with Poland. The marriage produced a son, Sigismund, who became King of both Sweden and Poland. A civil war broke out later when Sigismund's uncle, Charles, the Duke of Södermanland, took up the cause of Protestantism and the centralized state in opposition to Sigismund who was supported by the Catholics and the higher nobility and who favoured a more old-fashioned type of decentralized state controlled by the latter. The Finnish Governor, Klaus Fleming, and most of the Finnish nobility supported the King in this dispute and were later to pay for this when the Duke won the war and became King Charles IX. In what is known as the Club (i.e. cudgel) War (1596–97), Charles was supported by the peasants of Ostrobothnia, Tavastia and Savo, who discontented with the deterioration in social conditions, rose up in rebellion. The rebellion, however, was put down by Klaus

A portrait of Gustavus II Adolphus, framed by the coats of arms of the Swedish provinces. The order in which the coats of arms appear (those provinces which were later to become Finland do not form a separate group) show that Sweden and Finland were one Kingdom.

The title page of the first Finnish Grammar, compiled by Eskil Petraeus. The work was printed in Turku in 1649.

※※※※※※※※※※※※

LINGUÆ FINNICÆ
BREVIS
INSTITU-
TIO,

Exhibens vocum flectiones per Ca-
fus, Gradus & Tempora, nec non partium
indeclinabilium fignificationem, dictio-
numq; conftructionem &
Profodiam.

A D

Ufum accommodata.

Auguftinus ferm. de Tempore 186.
Tom. 10.pag. 230.

Nunquid modò fratres, non datur Spiritus ſanctus?
Quiſquis hoc putat, non eſt dignus accipere. Datur & modò. Quare ergo nemo loquitur lin-
gvis omnium gentium, ſicut loquebantur illi, qui tunc
Spiritu Sancto implebantur? Quare? Quia, quod
illud ſignificabat, impletum eſt.

A B O Æ,

Imprimebat Petrus Wald/An. 1649.

31

The Fleming family's
Louhisaari Manor is a rare
example of its kind in
Finland. Centralization in
the 17th century led to the
leading families of the
Kingdom building their
palaces in Stockholm and
their manors in the nearby
provinces.

Fleming.

During the reign of Gustavus II Adolphus, son
of Charles IX, war with Russia broke out once
more with the states bordering on Russia
attempting to take advantage of the country's
internal disorder. During this war, which ended

in 1617, Sweden annexed Ingria and the
province of Käkisalmi, areas which it had
temporarily held earlier. This left Russia
completely cut off from the Baltic Sea.

The 16th century was characterized by
attempts to strengthen the position of the

Crown and to centralize state administration. So successfully did Gustavus Vasa augment his position that in 1544 the system of elected kings was replaced with an hereditary monarchy. The centralization of tax collection and state finances made for considerable conformity, a development which was further strengthened by the transference to the state of the power and property of the Church. The struggle for power which followed when Gustavus Vasa bestowed Dukedoms on his sons (John was given the Duchy of Finland, i.e. the south-western part of the country, where, for a short period, he held what was for the times a magnificent Renaissance court in the Turku Castle) held back attempts at centralization. A struggle for power between the King and members of the higher nobility as well as a peasant rebellion brought about by the burden of a new administration and war machinery were common features in Europe at this time. As the Crown grew in strength it attempted to turn the nobility, which was a more or less independent local gentry, into a body of civil servants and military officials. The execution of many of Sigismund's followers went a long way towards breaking the power of the nobility. On the other hand, the continuous wars tended to stress the significance of the nobility, and by rewarding successful military leaders with prizes of land a kind of post-feudal situation was brought about. The change in the position of the nobility can be seen from the fact that, whereas in the latter part of the 16th century a number of Finland's leading families, including the Flemings and the Horns, had palatial mansions built, in the 17th century, with the exception of the Fleming family's Louhisaari and the Creutz' Sarvilahti, such extravagant family manors were not built at all in Finland. The powerful figures of the country tended to build their manors and palaces in or around Stockholm.

The Great Power

From the reign of Gustavus II Adolphus onwards, a characteristic feature of Sweden's period as a great power was the fact that, at first the Baltic countries, then Poland and finally Germany took the place of Russia as objects of Sweden's military and political ambitions. The wars in Germany were fought mainly with native Swedish manpower and this placed a considerable strain on the country's economy and population. This period of military activity, together with involvement in the wars on the continent, enhanced the position of the military leaders, that is to say the nobility. The Regency governments and the favourable attitudes of Queen Christina increased still further the prestige of the nobility. Many of those areas whose taxes were distributed as rewards for military achievements in the form of *fiefs* were located in Ostrobothnia and Karelia.

Another development during this period was the increasing importance attached to the position of Stockholm. With Stockholm the final home of central administration and with the Diet firmly rooted there through the erection of the first parliament building, the House of Nobility, the town exerted an influence on all parts of the Kingdom. Stockholm's position was also strengthened by a mercantile economic policy, one expression of which was the banning of foreign trade in towns along the Gulf of Finland and Gulf of Bothnia in favour of the capital. Thus the country's period as a great power saw the creation of a firmer administrative unity, a development that was felt in all walks of life.

During this period the main centres of population and the economic hub of the Kingdom of Sweden were situated around the waterways along the line Gothenburg–Stockholm–Turku–Tallin–Wiborg. At the beginning of the 17th century the emphasis was further to the east than it would be later, as is indicated by the fact that the two universities established after that of Uppsala were situated in Tarto (1632) and Turku (1640). Income received from Estonia and Lithuania was of considerable importance to the Kingdom. The composition of the ruling class was also altered with the intake of nobility from the Baltic countries. During the 1630's, with the war being waged for the most part in the south, the southern reaches of the Kingdom gained in importance and the inclusion in the realm of wealthy provinces seized from Denmark in 1658 meant that the country's centre of gravity shifted further west and further south. But it was not until the 18th century that Finland became a more peripheral region within the Kingdom. This was due, on the one hand, to the powerful growth of Gothenburg and trade with the west, and on the other, and this was more important, to Russian expansion westwards since the time of Peter the Great.

The establishment of a university (1640) and a Court of Appeals (1623) in Turku, the publication in Finnish of the complete Bible (1642) and the appearance of several new towns gives some indication of developments in Finland in the 17th century, a period during which the country was, on several occasions, to enjoy the status of a special area of administration. Count Per Brahe, Finland's Governor-General, did much to advance the country's position. In being placed under the administration of a Governor-General, Finland was not, in fact, treated as a special case within the Kingdom, as other parts of the realm were also liable to be temporarily grouped into a district of special administration. During his first period of office, Brahe's area of

Designed in the 1720's, after a long war, the town of Hamina
was built to defend the new border with Russia. The radial town
plan draws on Renaissance theories of the ideal town and on
Vauban's ideas on fortification.

administration comprised Finland and the province of Käkisalmi but not Ostrobothnia while his second covered Finland and Ostrobothnia without the province of Käkisalmi. This is one indication of the fact that the name Finland had not yet taken on its present meaning.

There was a good deal of migration between the various parts of the Kingdom, and this had its effect on the relationship between the two languages. Since the Middle Ages Finns from the west had been moving into Sweden and at the beginning of the 17th century large numbers of people migrated from Savo to western Sweden, where they gradually became absorbed into the Swedish-speaking population. Furthermore, centralization and the increased significance of Stockholm tended to strengthen the position of the Swedish language in Finland. Now and then, however, some attention was paid to the question of the ability of authorities in the Finnish-speaking area to use Finnish, and in the 18th century a translator was appointed to the Diet (the legislative assembly) for the benefit of the peasant representatives. In Stockholm, alongside the *Storkyrkan,* the Capital's most important church, there was also a Finnish church, which in fact still functions to this day. But it must be pointed out that, as the language of the Court and the nobility, German held an important position, as did Latin in University life.

Russian Expansion Westwards in the 18th Century

Changes along the eastern border, tension and a relative decline in her importance within the Kingdom were features central to developments in Finland during the 18th century. As Russia grew in strength it began to expand to the west and in 1703 St. Petersburg was founded on territory that was still formally part of Sweden. In the Great Northern War which began in 1700, Russia occupied Estonia and Lithuania in addition to Ingria and Karelia and, from 1710 onwards, the whole of Finland as far as the Åland Islands and was even threatening the archipelago around Stockholm. The period of occupation, which was to be known as the Great Wrath, came to end with the Peace of Uusikaupunki (Nystad) in 1721 and with it came a re-definition of the Kingdom's eastern border and for Finland (without Karelia) once more under Swedish rule, a more peripheral position than before.

Following the major famine of the 1690's, a long war and a period of occupation, Finland's population and agriculture were in a poor state but, after the Treaty of Uusikaupunki, rural areas experienced a rapid revival, particularly the agricultural sector. The population of the area later to be known as Finland was about 390 000 in 1721, but by 1807 it had grown to 907 000. Development in the towns and in

urban occupations was much slower. Despite a great number of new farms there was a rapid increase in the landless population and social divisions began to appear with a tenant-farmer class emerging on the one hand and a group of wealthy peasants and *rusthollis* (holder of a farm under obligation to furnish and equip a cavalryman) on the other. Particularly towards the latter half of the 18th century there was a general improvement in the standard of living and this was naturally reflected in the sphere of culture.

During the war of reprisal known as the War of the Hats, between 1741 and 1743, Finland was once more occupied by Russia. Under the Treaty of Turku (1743), with the new border drawn along the River Kymi, Finland lost the Olavinlinna fortress along with the towns of Lappeenranta and Hamina, the latter of which had been built up as a port and fortress town to replace Wiborg, ceded to Russia under the Treaty of Uusikaupunki. At this time the idea was already being expressed that Finland should break away from Sweden. However, after the war, measures were taken to strengthen Finland's position within the realm,

The Petäjävesi church (1763−64) in central Finland is a fine example of the technique and sense of form of Finnish church builders. They adapted remote architectural principles, which often arrived in Finland via Sweden, to suit the wooden materials at hand.

prominent among which were an economic development programme and the building of fortifications and a naval fleet. The construction of Sveaborg (Viapori in Finnish nowadays Suomenlinna) outside of Helsinki was a huge financial enterprise. Its very name indicates its wide national function. Economically and culturally Finland formed closer and closer links with Stockholm. Along with improvements in the standard of living and culture and better communications the Swedish language became more general. The effect of internal migration was felt particularly in the towns along the coast. A body of Finnish literature, mostly ecclesiastical and legal in nature, began to appear and for a short period a

---

The Fagervik forge-manor (main building 1773) in western Uusimaa was an important centre of both the early metal industry and horticulture.

The tomb of Augustin Ehrensvärd, founder of the Viapori Fortress, in the courtyard of Susisaari Castle. The tomb bears the inscription: here rests Count August Ehrensvärd, Field-Marshal, Knight and Commander of His Royal Majesty's Order, surrounded by His Work, the Fortress of Sveaborg, the Army Fleet. − The draft design for the tomb was drawn by Gustavus III and it was completed by Tobias Sergel.

Count Gustaf Mauritz Armfelt's study in Åminne Manor. Armfelt had the ear of both Gustavus III of Sweden and Alexander I of Russia. After 1809 he played a central part in the creation of a new state during Finland's period as a Grand Duchy.

Finnish-language newspaper was published. The position of the Finnish language was recognized in the Diet and on bank notes, etc. but the increasing importance of the western parts of the Kingdom, including Gothenburg, pushed the whole of Finland and consequently the Finnish language into a more peripheral position. This was the main reason for the fact that the Finnish civil service became continuously more Finnish, that is to say that fewer and fewer officials came to Finland from other parts of the Kingdom.

The Regency, which reached the peak of its power towards the end of the 17th century, was superseded by the power of the Estates, the "Age of Freedom", which, in turn, came to an end with Gustavus III's coup d'état in 1772. The reign of Gustavus III and Gustavian culture were to be of importance to Finland and the reaffirmation of the power of the Regency was regarded as serving Finnish interests better than the power of the Diet. However, the nobility gradually rose up in opposition to the King as he began to limit the power of the Diet, simultaneously favouring those Estates of lower economic status. This development reached its peak in 1789 with the Act of Union and Security which was in the nature of a constitution and which the King sprang on the Diet as a kind of *fait accompli* in the middle of the war against Russia (1788–90).

During this war, which also developed into a

war against Denmark, a separatist movement among army officers, with its roots in the opposition formed by the nobility, attempted to force the King to make peace by conducting separate negotiations with Russia. The origins of this officers' revolt (they were called the Anjala League) lay partly in plans, outlined a few years earlier by G.M. Sprengtporten, for an independent Finland under Russian suzerainty: these plans envisaged a nobility-centred form of government, based on ideas from the United States of America, resembling the Diet of the Age of Freedom. While they probably played a part in the way Finland's position would be organized between 1808 and 1809, these plans received little support during the war of 1788−1790.

But it is difficult to draw parallels between Finland's position as it was envisaged under Russian rule, with its government of nobles, and the reality of the country's subsequent history. Behind these events, which were tied up with the Anjala League, was the broad national constitutional opposition of the nobility to the power of the Regency. On the other hand, from Russia's point of view the plans to separate Finland from Sweden were of great significance. Following the subsequent Finnish war (1808−1809), fought against the background of the European power politics of the Napoleonic era, occupied Finland was no longer handed back to Sweden as it had been in

1721 and 1743, but was annexed by Russia as an autonomous "buffer state" with its own Diet and administration; Russia had, in fact, already considered the establishment of such a Diet during earlier periods of occupation in the 18th century. However, as the war indicates, there was a great deal of opposition to partition in Sweden and Finland. The reasons for Finland's separation from Sweden were not based on ethnical or linguistic principles or on the kind of nationalistic grounds that would appear later, neither was the border between Sweden and Russia (the Finnish Grand Duchy) drawn up on the basis of ethnic-linguistic considerations. It was not until after 1809 that a sense of Finnish identity began to develop, a trend which was later to embrace the kind of antiquarian interest that H.G. Porthan and his friends and pupils were to show in Finnish history, folklore and language during the latter part of the 18th century when the influence of the old University of Turku had been at its peak.

The Autonomous Grand Duchy

In signing the Treaty of Tilsit in 1807, Czar Alexander I of Russia and Napoleon had come to an agreement on their respective spheres of interest, after which Russia had conquered Finland (1808—1809). Finland was of strategic importance to Russia because of its proximity to St. Petersburg. A hundred years earlier Peter the Great had conquered Karelia, Estonia and Lithuania and had founded his Capital on the territory he had taken. It was logical, therefore, to attempt to make the entire Gulf of Finland inaccessible to enemy fleets. Russia's front line of defence was brought up from Kronstadt to the Sveaborg (Suomenlinna) fortifications and even further to the west. In the 1830's work was begun on what was planned to be the major fortification of Bomarsund on the Åland Islands. With its sparse population and its poverty, Finland as such did not interest Russia, but the establishment of St Petersburg had made it necessary to protect its western capital and ensure access to the Baltic Sea. Sweden, its period as a great power at an end, no longer constituted any great danger; but what Russia did consider a danger was the possibility that during a major war Sweden, or later an independent Finland, by forming alliances with Russia's enemies, would provide them with a base from which to attack. It was Sweden's alliance with Great Britain, the enemy of France and Russia, (now enjoying friendly relations), that was behind the war of 1808—1809.

A very important aspect of Russia's

annexation of Finland was the way in which it was carried out and the form that Finnish society assumed as a result. As such, it was not exceptional that Finland was allowed to retain its own legislation and its own form of society since many other countries annexed by Russia earlier, including the Baltic states, had kept their own forms of government and in 1815 Poland too retained its status as a separate kingdom within the Russian Empire. Finland's position was confirmed, with the war still in progress, at the Grand Duchy's first separate Diet held in Porvoo, at which time the Czar proclaimed Finland's "elevation to the national status". Russia was not a united centralized state, neither was it united nationally or religiously. Thus, from the Russian point of view there was nothing peculiar or exceptional in Finland's Lutheran Church. However, in relation to Russia, Finland's position regarding its internal affairs was one of considerable independence, evidently for the reason that, in certain respects, it served as a model area from the point of view of the liberal policies that Alexander I was pursuing at the time. The free status of the Finnish peasantry and their

---

The old city of Turku in the year 1814. Before the fire of Turku in 1827 the Cathedral had a bulbous dome at the top of its baroque tower and was surrounded by tightly-packed buildings of which only a few remain. In the foreground a group of Russian soldiers and a sentry-box.

F. Tengström's lithograph of Helsinki's Senate Square in the
year 1838. At this time St. Nicholas' Church (now the
Cathedral) was still as C.L. Engel had designed it. In the 1840's
several additions were made, including its corner towers, and

the Main Guard Building in front of the church was replaced with monumental steps. The University on the left and the University Library in the background have remained unchanged.

representation in the Diet was of particular importance to Alexander and his plans to carry out reforms throughout the Realm, plans which were interrupted by Napoleon's attack in 1812. Finland not only retained its Lutheran religion, Swedish as its official language, its old Swedish system of civil and criminal law, but also its Gustavian form of government, the adaptation of which to Finnish circumstances together with the fact that Finland had its own central administration headed by the Senate and, in principle, its own Diet with its four Estates, meant the birth of a separate Finnish state. Finland had, of old, held the heraldic status of a Grand Duchy, now it became a Grand Duchy de facto, with its own institutions. The autocratic Czar of Russia agreed, by way of an "experiment" to become the constitutional monarch of Finland and Poland. From here it was intended that this system be extended to cover the whole of Russia. However, due to changing circumstances in Europe this did not materialize and, as a result of the uprisings in 1830 and 1863, Poland lost its Parliament and its special status. The Finns, who remained loyal and rather conservative throughout the 19th century, had what were on the whole

---

The Helsinki University Library (1836–45) seen from the Cathedral: this majestically proportioned building is considered by many to be C.L. Engel's best work. The central dome covers one of the finest interiors in the country.

rather favourable conditions to develop a state which had come into being as the result of Great Power politics and which, although it did not constitute an ethnic totality, was neverthless a geographically viable entity. Dialects of Finnish were spoken on both the Swedish and Russian sides of the border and, in Finland itself, in addition to the Swedish-speaking or bi-lingual upper classes, there was a

Werner Holmberg: Storm over Lake Näsijärvi. Holmberg, who died young, was creating in his paintings the same kind of idealized picture of Finnish nature that Runeberg and Topelius created in their poetry.

considerable Swedish-speaking rural population. Alexander had wanted the state to include the Swedish-speaking Åland Islands but not the Finnish-speaking area of Länsipohja (Westrobothnia); what was involved was the forming of a strategic and not expressly an ethnic entity. As far as trade and communications were concerned, western Finland inclined towards Sweden, Eastern ·

Finland more and more towards St Petersburg. Later, the network of roads and canals, and particularly the coming of the railroad, would support the tendency of administration to centralize in a way counter to the disintegrative hull of these major commercial centres.

A clear indication of Russia's desire to make an independently functioning entity of Finland was the creation of the area's own Capital. Under Swedish rule, Turku, with its Bishop's Seat, its University and its Court of Appeals, had been the centre of the province, but Finland's Capital had, of course, been Stockholm. Now, with the decision to make Helsinki the new administrative centre, a new Capital was created. Helsinki had been burnt down during the war and now it was re-built in an unprecedentedly handsome fashion to show both Finns and the outside world that a new political unit, the Grand Duchy of Finland, had come into being. It was then that those institutions and, to a great extent, the buildings which still today house Finland's central administration were created. The President of the Republic, of course, resides in the former palace of the Czar.

The building up and the preservation of Finland's institutions and her special status was

J.L. Runeberg hunting with his sons and dogs in the Finnish archipelago.

the oldest bureaucratic means of forming a national identity. With the exception of a Governor-General, the representative of the Czar, the Finnish civil service was composed entirely of native Finns. But it was only with the convening of the Diet that wider circles could make themselves felt. The Diet, which had assembled only once before, in Porvoo in 1809, was convened again in 1863 during Alexander II's period of liberalization, and from then on at regular intervals. With Europe experiencing a period of political reaction, Finland came under the severe and patriarchal rule of Czar Nicholas I. But Nicholas respected Finland's special status and during his reign a number of writers whose work went a long way to creating a sense of national unity in Finland emerged alongside the bureaucracy. J.L. Runeberg, Finland's national poet, in such works as *Elk Hunting on Skis* and *Tales of Ensign Stål* created an idealized picture of a poor but industrious Finnish people living in harmony and contentment. These works contain an elevated but humane and often humorous description of the people, and includes what was to become the Finnish national anthem, "Maamme" (Our Land), in which the beauty of Finland's summer landscape becomes the

Runeberg's home in Porvoo. Runeberg was recognized in his own lifetime as Finland's first Great Man.

Elias Lönnrot, the great collector of ancient Finnish folk poems, journalist and publisher of the Finnish national epic the Kalevala. Lönnrot was well known for his modesty and warm-hearted humour. This caricature shows him as a bare-footed country wanderer. The text reads: Unus homo nobis cursando restituit rem.

object of love of the fatherland. Alongside the works of Runeberg, the body of Finnish folklore collected and presented in poetic form by Elias Lönnrot was to be of the greatest significance. This collection, the Finnish national Epic, the *Kalevala,* did much to spread an awareness of Finland's existence and special character throughout Europe in spite of the fact that, from the point of view of the emergent Finnish culture and even the Finnish language, the folklore on which it is based played a peripheral and receding role. It was not so much the contents or the language of the Kalevala which gave its publication such importance but the fact that Finns had been capable of such a cultural achievement. As distinct from Sweden, Finland had no history of its own, and (in a Romantic age, in which history, the Gothic and old ruins played an important role in the emergence of a national identity in many other countries) very few historical monuments. Thus Runeberg's "antique" concept of man and his idealization of the Finnish landscape together with the existence of the Kalevala were long to form the basis of a sense of Finnish national identity. It was only at the turn of the century that the *Kalevala,* as a source of inspiration to the masters of the "Golden Age" of Finnish art, was to have an important impact on Finnish culture.

The fact that the country had only one University to train the entire future civil service

was an important factor in bringing about Finnish unity. The University held a central position in the country's intellectual life since outside its circles cultural resourses were few. There were, after all, no large cities and no wealthy bourgeoisie, the nobility was small in number and the clergy was dispersed throughout the country. However, the University, which received the strong support of the government, did provide the prerequisites for literary and scientific study and the organizations connected to the University were the only forums in which political debate was possible. Thus the University fulfilled an important function in training and supplying the human capital for the critical years of the 1860's. A considerable proportion of the staff of the new Diet, of the journalists of the political and literary press and even of those people involved in creating a new era in art and industry were products of the University.

Along with the University, another important educational channel during Finland's period of autonomy was the Imperial Army. At the beginning of the 19th century one in five sons of the nobility, later one in nine, served in the Russian army, as did many outside the nobility, and Finland had its own Cadet School. The fact

Colonel C.G.E. Mannerheim, commanding officer of the 13th Uhlan Regiment in the Russian Imperial army. The regiment was stationed in Poland.

A woodcut from the 1870's showing the Saimaa canal which was opened in 1856. Before the coming of the railway the canal was an important means of transportation, opening up a channel between the lake district and the sea and having a strong

influence on trade in eastern Finland. In modern Finland it is still possible to find such idyllic canal settings in which the work of man and nature combine in harmony. But young scarf-clad girls selling strawberries are nowadays a rarity.

that about four hundred out of a total of some 3000 Finnish soldiers are known to have reached the rank of General or Admiral is a measure of their success. Many of these soldiers returned to Finland to take up posts in the civil

---

The English and French fleet bombarded the Viapori fortifications in 1855 during the Crimean war. This is a French lithograph based on the events as described by a war correspondent. Pictures of Viapori published in England and France often depict the fortifications as a real Gibraltar of the North.

service or to work in industry or other professions. Their period of service and the high-level training they received in different positions in the army of what was perhaps the most powerful state in the world brought the kind of insight and experience to Finland that did much to prevent the intellectual isolation which otherwise threatens a small country. The most well known figure to have chosen this path was the Finnish Field-Marshal, Mannerheim.

In spite of its autonomy Finland was not separated from Russia in other respects. Men

from the local Russian garrisons were common sights in many Finnish towns. Along with them came Russian merchants and through their influence Orthodox churches were built. On the other hand there was a constant flow of people from eastern Finland to St Petersburg where they either settled permanently or returned a few years later. The St Petersburg economy, in other ways too, had a great influence on Finland.

The reign of Alexander II (1855−81), and in particular the 1860's, was a period of considerable liberalization in Finland, where reforms went on even after Russia itself had turned in a more conservative direction. The most important reform concerned the Diet. Following the convening of a preparatory committee in January 1861, the Diet of 1863−64 was held in Helsinki as were all subsequent ones. The rules of procedure for the Diet, which contained Four Estates until 1906, were enacted in 1869. Thus, at the beginning of the century, the bureaucratic society was being replaced by a civic society, one in which, it is true, the right to vote in matters of state was extended to only a very small section of the people, depending on the composition of the various Estates. The change-over to a new form of society was advanced by decrees granting self-administration to the provinces, universal freedom to ply a trade, permission to establish banks and limited companies, equal rights of inheritance to women and by the removal of education from the control of the Church, as well as a great many other reforms. From the 1860's onwards the establishment of numerous companies, societies and newspapers heralded the arrival of a new era.

The fact that new forms of livelihood were encouraged can be seen not only in the legislation of the time but also in policies regarding transport and communications. At the beginning of the 19th century, with the purchasing of coastal steamers and the building of canals, great strides were made in developing water traffic. The Saimaa Canal, an important Finnish waterway, was opened in 1856. Towards the end of the century an extensive network of railways was built, its main lines connecting Helsinki—Riihimäki—Wiborg-St Petersburg, and with branch lines to Ostrobothnia (from Helsinki to Hämeenlinna as early as 1862), Savo, Karelia, Hanko and Turku. Internal migration, along with the transportation of goods, followed the direction of the railways. The "surplus population" of the inland areas of eastern Finland and Ostrobothnia moved to the rapidly growing city of Helsinki, to the industrial areas along the River Kymijoki, to the new port of Kotka, to Wiborg and Tampere, providing these areas with an industrial labour force. There was also a good deal of migration from eastern Finland to St Petersburg and emigration to America,

Tampere in the 1860's: later to be called the Manchester of Finland, it became, at the end of the 19th century, Finland's first industrial town. Nowadays the factories beside the rapids are seen as a monument to the early history of industrialism but Tampere has to a great extent retained its industrial character.

mostly from Ostrobothnia. For a long time to come industrial workers would be few compared to the number of those working in agriculture but the compact environment of the towns facilitated the formation of workers' social and political associations – a typical feature of a newly industrializing and urbanizing society. Another feature typical of the times was the increasing importance of international trade and cultural exchange. The change-over to the metric system between the years 1887 and 1892 (a move which took place in Russia and Finland earlier than in many western European countries) can be seen as a sign of the significance of international commerce.

The fact that Finland had its own Diet, its own army and its own unit of currency, the Mark (it was introduced in 1860, released from its ties with the Ruble in 1865 and tied to the gold standard in 1878), had an important effect on the country's political and economic life and on the process of modernization, as well as having the greatest significance, both inside Finland and abroad, as symbols of the country's autonomy and internal self-government, particularly in view of the fact that Russia itself had no Parliament of its own and that the fiscal situation of the Russian Empire was less stable than that of Finland. As time went by the reforms brought about in Finland and the privileges gained there became the object of unfavourable attention in Russia, especially because of their symbolic significance but also because of commercial competition. As the international political situation changed Finland's position began to be more difficult. When, in 1871, Bismarck created a strong German state and relations between Germany and Russia later on grew more distant, Finland found itself in a sensitive strategic position. Criticism of Finland's political and economic autonomy and the country's links with the West, began to be expressed in Russia.

During the early stages of Finland's autonomy it had been natural for Russia to support attempts to create a separate Finnish culture since this would serve to insulate the Finns from the Swedes. It would follow that, if Sweden tried to regain control of Finland, the Finns would not join the Swedes but would defend themselves and in so doing defend the Empire. During the Crimean War in the 1850's Sweden did in fact come close to allying itself to England and France who were active in the Baltic Sea and bombarding the coast of Finland. With the exception of a few liberal students the Finns demonstrated their solidarity with Russia in this situation. Nicholas I (whose reign is so often considered to have represented a period of reaction) had no reason, for example, to prevent the birth of the Society of Finnish Literature in 1831. It was during Nicholas' reign, in fact, that first a Finnish language lectureship (1828) and later a professorship (1850) were established at the University and this was at a time when new posts for lecturers in languages and particularly for professors were very rare indeed at universities anywhere. In the 1840's it began to be required that Finnish civil servants show proof of their command of the Finnish language and, in 1863, Czar Alexander II made Finnish an official language of administration and legal proceedings. In 1850, on the other hand, in order to prevent the circulation of political literature following the year of revolution in Europe (1848–49), the government placed a temporary restriction on publications in Finnish. The use of Finnish as a language of administration developed at the same time as the rise of a Finnish literary culture. Thus the press, on both languages, took on importance only in connection with the liberal breakthrough of the 1860's. The lack of intellectual resourses in Finland and not a conservative government policy, therefore, was the main obstacle to the growth of a Finnish-language culture. All in all the educated class was rather small which meant that it took a long time before they were able to create anything of a durable nature. This was

The statue of Alexander II in Helsinki's Senate Square. It is the work of J.L. Runeberg's son, Walter, one of Finland's leading sculptors at the end of the 19th century.

true of both language groups. In Finland there were not, in fact, two distinct cultures, one Finnish-speaking and one Swedish-speaking: as far as output was concerned both cultures were essentially the same. The Finnish-speaking culture had long been dependent on the Swedish but, in terms of ideology, the Swedish-speaking culture was just as Finnish as the Finnish one itself. This ideology had been created by Runeberg, Lönnrot, Fredrik Cygnaeus, Snellman, Topelius and their contemporaries. Such figures as Yrjö-Koskinen and Julius Krohn (Suonio), who were responsible for much of the Finnish-speaking culture, had been brought up in Swedish-speaking and sometimes German-speaking environments. Many members of the educated class began quite voluntarily to use Finnish. The transition from one cultural language to another took place relatively slowly and smoothly. Generally speaking the question of language placed no national or social limits on the bi-lingual educated class. The bi-lingual tradition has

---

The young Jean Sibelius painted by his brother-in-law Eero Järnefelt in 1892. The 26-year-old Sibelius had achieved his first success as composer of the Kullervo Symphony which was based on a story from the Kalevala. Although the Kullervo Symphony was to disappear from the composer's repertoire for as long as Sibelius lived (until 1958), it marked the beginning of his early nationalist period.

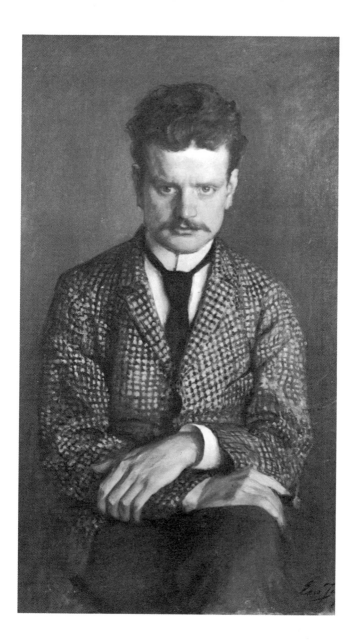

Albert Edelfelt: The Luxembourg Gardens (1887). Edelfelt and
his contemporaries gradually turned away from the
Scandinavian and German tradition and looked more and more
towards Paris. Edelfelt himself was an international figure both

in his art and in his personal relations and was one of the leading names in Finnish art at the end of the 19th and beginning of the 20th centuries.

been very strong in Finland and its culture, lasting at least until the second World War and is still, of course, very important today. This tradition has also kept Finland in close touch with the culture of Scandinavia.

The formation of interest groups into political parties, a process which had begun in the 1860's, was partly the result of disputes over the position of the languages. The national and social programme of the Fennoman Party, in particular (the party was led by Professor G.Z. Forsman, who wrote under the name of Yrjö Koskinen and was later elevated to the ranks of the nobility and given the title Baron Yrjö-Koskinen) was closely linked with demands for improvements in the position of the Finnish language, culture and economy. But, here too, what was involved was an entire programme which can be said to have represented, for the most part, the values and interests of the rural population, put forward in a spirit of national idealism and a kind of social conservatism. At this time the party was not an organization as such but consisted of a group of interests, supporting certain opinions, whose ranks included the majority of the clergy and the peasantry in the Diet, Finnish Clubs and Societies in many towns, almost the entire Finnish press, which was expanding rapidly at the time, and a good half of the student bodies, especially those representing the inland areas. In the 1890's the Fennoman Party was split into two when a nationalist-liberal faction of "Young Finns" with the daily newspaper *Päivälehti* (1889, Helsingin Sanomat since 1904) as its spearhead, set themselves in opposition to the "Old Finns" led by Yrjö-Koskinen and the newspaper *Uusi Suometar.*

The other party grouping comprised the majority of the nobility and the bourgeoisie in the Diet, student bodies representing the coastal areas, representatives of trade and industry and, in general, supporters of liberal ideas. This movement, whose most important supporter was the newspaper *Helsingfors Dagblad* (1862–89, said to be Finland's first modern newspaper) and of whose leaders the most well known was Leo Mechelin, later joined ranks with a group representing the Swedish-national ideal known as the "Viking Group", particularly after attempts by the liberals to form their own political party in 1880 had failed. Opposition to the language programme of the Fennoman Party was based largely on a desire to safeguard the standard of Finnish culture and out of concern for cultural links with the West and the basic precepts of constitutional politics. Swedish-language nationalism took on importance only when, following the Parliamentary reforms at the beginning of the 20th century, the appeal of the Swedish People's Party, founded in 1906, began to widen to include the rural Swedish-speaking population.

During the latter half of the 19th century great changes occurred in rural conditions. An increase in the value of wood led, as a result of trade in timber, to a change from a subsistence agricultural economy to a monetary economy, widening the gap in the standard of living between those who owned forests and those who did not, with the latter losing their rights to the use of forest land. Rural conditions and the distribution of wealth were particularly affected by modernizations in agriculture — the development of methods of cultivation and cattle raising requiring greater capital outlay and producing larger profits. Cheap imported grain led to the domestic market concentrating on cattle farming and the exporting of butter. Farmers were able to increase their standard of living manyfold, renew their building stock, educate their children and purchase modern farming equipment, but only small changes were brought about in the conditions of the landless population and the difference between their standard of living and that of the landowners increased rapidly. The landless population comprised cottagers, who lived in rented cottages but had no land of their own, hired farm-hands, who lived in and were dependent on the farm house, as well as tenant farmers, who rented farm-land but were obliged to work for the landowner when he so required. A great many of the rural population (their numbers had grown considerably throughout the century) moved to the towns to work in industry or emigrated. It was the rural proletariat which suffered most during the years of crop-failures and particularly during the famine of 1867−68. There was an awareness that reforms were necessary to improve the conditions of the rural landless, but changes did not occur. In the first Parliamentary elections to embrace universal suffrage in 1907 it was the rural proletariat that guaranteed the enormous success of the radical Social Democratic Party. However, in the face of opposition from the Czar and the government, Parliament could not put reforms into effect, a situation which led to the social tension that was an important feature in Finland at the turn of the century.

Along with tension on the domestic front came increased tension between Finland and Russia. The growing power of the German state led to a military alliance between Russia and France at the beginning of the 1890's and the strategic importance of Finland's south coast became greater. While improvements in Finland's defence and system of railways were undertaken to meet the changing situation, greater and greater attention was being paid in Russia to the question of whether the Finnish people were still as loyal and trustworthy as they had been throughout the 19th century. In purely commercial terms Finland had already

The Finnish pavilion at the Paris World Fair in 1900. Drawing
its inspiration from Finnish nationalism and the international
art nouveau movement the building earned a great deal of
attention and respect for the distant Grand Duchy: the World
Fair represented a great step forward into international
prominence for Finnish national art. The interior of the
pavilion's Iris room was designed by Akseli Gallen-Kallela. The
furniture was made under the supervision of the Swedish
Count, Louis Sparre, at what was to become the famous Iris
factory in Porvoo.

formed such strong ties with the West that her ties with Russia might be called into question, and strong cultural development was drawing Finland closer to Europe than to Russia. Russia made attempts to bring Finland more firmly back into its sphere of influence particularly in important military areas. But this led to conflict between the Russian government and the upper strata of Finnish society.

In 1898 the determined Russian General Nikolai Ivanovich Bobrikov became Governor-General of Finland. The Manifesto of February, 1899, which was rather general in nature, represented his attempts to bring Finland back to the Russian fold. Faced with this situation, leading circles in Finland, particularly the alliance between the Swedish-minded Liberals and the "Young" Fennomen, which later formed the basis of the Constitutional or Opposition group, began to put up a concerted opposition. By making appeals to humanitarian and legal circles and by publicizing the achievements of Finnish culture and industry at such venues as the Paris World Fair in 1900, a great deal of attention was drawn to the Finnish question in Scandinavia, Germany and the western world in general. At home, public opinion was organized on a wider basis with the collection and presentation to the Czar of a "Grand Petition" signed by half a million Finns and especially by opposition to a law designed to conscript Finns into the Russian army. There were deep differences of opinion, however, as to what attitude should be taken to Russian aims. The "Old" Fennomen, in particular, favoured a strategy of negotiations aimed, primarily, at keeping the Senate and the administrative machinery in Finnish hands. The opposition, the Constitutionalists, saw this as following a line of submission. The "Old" Fennomen became embittered at doubts thrown on their patriotism for remaining in the Senate when their opponents resigned. Bobrikov's period, which is known emotionally as the "years of oppression", came to an end with his assassination in summer, 1904 and to a political conclusion with the general strike of autumn, 1905.

With Russia losing the war with Japan and the Czar obliged to agree to the establishment of a system of popular representation in Russia, the government's policy towards Finland underwent a change. In Finland, the old Four-Estates Diet was replaced by a single-chamber Parliament in 1906. At a stroke Finland changed over from the oldest parliamentary system in Europe to the most modern. Under universal suffrage the number of voters in the country increased tenfold and Finland became the first country in Europe to extend the franchise to women. In the elections which followed, the Social Democratic Party, in which revolutionary views held an important position, gained 40 % of the mandate, its share

increasing in subsequent elections until, in
1916, the socialists gained a majority in
Parliament. The great reforms voted for in
Parliament were not put into effect, however, as
they were not ratified by the Czar and the

Jean Sibelius with his family in the drawing room of their home, Ainola, in Järvenpää in 1915. The simple interior of the building, designed by Lars Sonck, is reminiscent of the nationalist trend in the Arts but the composer had, more than ten years earlier, set out on the road from the national to the universal.

Russian government.

Following the general strike and a shift in government policy in Russia, decrees enacted in Bobrikov's time were repealed and a Senate led by Mechelin came into power. Despite its reform, the new Parliament had no constitutional basis which meant that the Senate and the Governor-General were dependent on the confidence of the Czar. In 1909, as the political situation changed, first

the Constitutionalists and later the Old"
Fennomen resigned from the Senate their place
being taken by pro-government civil-servants
who lacked the confidence of Parliament and
the political parties, and from 1912 onwards,

Albert Gebhard's painting of an orphan girl (1895) certainly
appealed powerfully to those Finns for whom the famine of
1868 or the question of the landless population and all that it
involved at the end of the century were serious social problems.

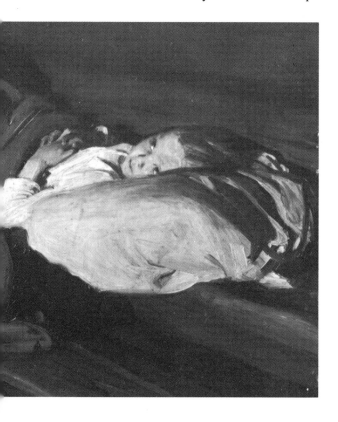

under a law giving equal status to Finnish and Russian subjects, by native Russians too. Finland's Governor-General from 1909 until the Revolution was General F.A. Seyn who was given the task of preventing the re-occurrence of such events as the general strike of 1905 and of thwarting Finnish and Russian revolutionary activities. This period of Finnish history is known as the second period of oppression but economically and culturally it was a fruitful time in many respects. It was also a time which saw, in addition to the growing tension in Finnish-Russian relations, a widening gap between bourgeois and socialist social groups. Under these conditions there was a growing desire, especially in Swedish-speaking quarters, to seek links with Sweden and, upon the outbreak of the first World War, with Germany. These aims are reflected in the fact that during the World War many young Finnish men volunteered to join not only the Russian army but also left to train as infantrymen in the army of the enemy, Germany and that, following the war, White Finland (the country was divided into White and Red camps) formed close contacts with the still fairly strong Imperial Germany.

Independent Finland

The Russian Revolution of March 1917
restored Finland to a position of autonomy. As
the spring progressed, however, many Finns
advanced the idea of complete independence
from Russia while still more were of the opinion
that Finland's future lay in the same kind of
autonomous position that it had held under
Russia in the 19th century. Those in favour of
separation included, for the most part, the
left-wing and the pro-German section of the
bourgeoisie. In summer 1917, the Finnish
Parliament, assumed the power that had been
vested in the Czar, but the Russian Provisional
Government under Alexander Kerenski,
dissolved the Finnish Parliament and the
enabling Act lapsed. These events widened the
gap between the bourgeoisie and the left who
had pushed through the Act. In the autumn
elections the balance of power in Parliament
changed with the bourgeoisie gaining a
majority and Parliament decided once more to
assume "supreme authority" since attitudes
towards Russia in bourgeois circles had been
changed once and for all by the October
Revolution. The so-called Independence
Senate, led by P.E. Svinhufvud proposed to
Parliament that Finland should declare
independence and that the new sovereign state

should be a Republic. The proposal was approved by Parliament on December 6th, 1917. Foreign powers were unwilling to recognize Finnish independence before the Soviet government had done so. On 31st December, 1917, upon the request of the Senate, Lenin's government announced its recognition of the new state, after which France, Sweden, Germany, Austro-Hungary, Greece, Norway and Denmark quickly followed suit; Great Britain and the United States, on the other hand, recognized Finland's independence only one and a half years later. Recognition of Finnish independence, however, did not mean the withdrawal of Soviet troops stationed in Finland in spite of attempts by the Finnish Senate to accomplish this.

The Socialists were no longer so eager to break with Russia. The radical left, hoping for a revolution in Finland too, achieved the ascendancy in the Social Democratic Party. At the end of January, 1918 the "Reds" took over power in Helsinki and southern Finland. The Senate fled to Vaasa in Ostrobothnia where

---

Wäinö Aaltonen was Finland's most important sculptor during the first ten years of independence. His monument in Savonlinna honouring the White soldiers killed in 1918 is an example of 1920's classicism reflecting the idealism of the young Republic.

they established a "White" stronghold controlling northern and central Finland. General Gustaf Mannerheim was called in to take control as commander-in-chief of the "White" forces and, at the beginning of April he won the decisive battle for Tampere. At the same time, at the invitation of the Senate, a German division landed on the south coast of Finland, taking Helsinki and other towns. The role played by the Germans in supporting the "Whites" and that of Russia in supplying arms and assistance to the "Reds" is a clear indication of the fact that, in addition to Finland's internal affairs, the war also involved the question of the spheres of interest of the Major Powers. At the outbreak of the first World War Germany had already attempted to pave the way to rebellion in Finland by training a group of Finnish volunteers as light-infantrymen. With the end of the war in spring 1918, Germany made efforts to tie Finland firmly to its sphere of interest. At the political level this is seen from the fact that the Kaiser's brother-in-law, Prince Friedrich Karl of Hessen, was elected King of Finland. Germany's collapse prevented him from ever ascending the throne, however, and at the same time Finland was freed from its economic and military alliance with Germany. Mannerheim, who had opposed the pro-German trend in Finland, became regent and under his leadership the country began to look towards the western world. On 17th July, 1919 the Constitution, which is still in force, was ratified by Mannerheim and Finland's relations with foreign states were normalized. Under a peace treaty signed with Russia at Tartu in 1920, the area of Petsamo in Lapland was added to Finland's former territory, which meant that the country now extended to the Arctic Ocean; Finland was later to lose this area under the armistice of 1944.

The Finnish Constitution was created as a compromise between republican and monarchist opinion. It left the President with most of the power enjoyed by the head of state under the previous constitution: responsibility for foreign policy, the position of Commander in Chief of the army and the right to dissolve Parliament. While the President's position within the system of state became of central importance, a multi-party system led to short-term governments varying in their political composition.

With the Constitution affording the President a central position in affairs of state, the first two Presidents of the Republic, K.J. Ståhlberg and L.Kr. Relander, both exercised their right to dissolve Parliament in the face of opposition from the Council of State. Neither did the next President, P.E. Svinhufvud adhere to the classical principles of democracy, with minority governments in power throught most of his term of office. By contrast K. Kallio's term of office was a period of government by broadly-based coalitions. Under R. Ryti, Finland's war-time President, and the three post-war Presidents, G. Mannerheim, J.K. Paasikivi and U.K. Kekkonen, the President's position as leader of the country's foreign policy has taken on an ever greater importance, a development which has naturally also affected Finland's internal affairs. While the President's position has been thrown into relief by the short duration of the various governments, the fact that the same individuals have held ministerial positions in successive governments has made for a certain continuity. Parliamentary elections have for a long time been fairly stable; the 1930's saw a growth in support for the Right, with a corresponding increase in support for the Left in the years immediately following the war. With the exception of Tanner's minority Social Democratic government (1926—1927) the 1920's was a period of government by centre and centre-right coalitions. The 1930's was a time of "Presidential" governments (foremost among which was the long-lived Kivimäki administration) until 1937 when, with K. Kallio becoming President, a Social Democrat—Agrarian—Progressive Party coalition came into power.

The greatest change to take place in the form of government since independence, apart from the change-over from a heriditary monarchy to a regularly elected head of state, was the

adoption of Parliamentary principles.
Otherwise Finland, unlike most other countries
achieving independence after World War I,
already had its own system of representation
and administration, elections by universal
suffrage, its own civil service and financial
institution, its own economy and culture.

The political significance of the war of 1918
lies in the fact that it determined whether
Finland would follow Russia on the road to
revolution. In the anti-revolutionary sense, in
removing Russian troops from Finland and
securing the country's political independence, it
was a "war of liberation" which came to a
conclusion at Tarto in 1920. As a "civil war" its
roots lay largely in the growing dissatisfaction
with social inequalities that had long been
smouldering beneath the surface. Soon after the
war the reforms which had long been planned
but which had been postponed because of
political circumstances, were put into effect.
The most important reform concerned the
finding of land for the landless population and
freeholds for tenant farmers.

During the early years of independence acts
were passed introducing compulsory education,
prohibition of alcohol (repealed in 1932),
freedom of worship, freedom of speech and
freedom to form societies. Legislation was
introduced regulating the position of the two
language groups and an Act was passed
providing autonomy for the Åland Islands, an

area over which Finnish sovereignty had been confirmed by the League of Nations and which had long represented a bone of contention between Finland and Sweden. During Ståhlberg's period as President, an Act of Amnesty was passed under which those convicted as leaders of the "Reds" were quickly pardoned in an attempt to dispel the destructive memories of the War in 1918. In the spring of 1919, the Social Democratic Party, the representative of the losing side in the war, could participate in the elections and became the largest party in Parliament. As early as 1926 the Social Democrats alone formed the Government, a fact which can be seen as an indication of the stabilization of the democratic system. This success is explained in part by the fact that the Left had split in two, with the Social Democrats representing the moderate wing of the old Socialist Party. The revolutionary wing founded the Finnish Communist Party in the Soviet Union in 1918, but this was illegal in Finland until 1944. Otherwise the Agrarian Party and the Swedish Party continued as before with the Finnish-speaking section of the bourgeoisie re-forming their ranks to fight over the constitutional form the country was to have. The monarchists formed the National Coalition Party which was made up for the most part of members of the "Old" Fennoman Party, while the Republicans formed the Progressive Party around a core of "Young" Fennomen. In addition to two other small parties, the Christian Party and a political group which fronted for the Communists, another party to emerge at this time was the Fascist-like Patriotic People's Movement (IKL). Founded in 1933, its early support soon dwindled and it was proscribed under the armistice of 1944.

In spite of many economic difficulties and a relatively low standard of living, a spirit of optimism prevailed in Finland throughout the 1920's, a mood which was heightened by the success of Finnish sportsmen, by the appearance of new literature, by the kind of international intercourse, with its diplomats and state visits, for which sovereignity is a prerequisite, and by Finland's participation in the League of Nations. On the other hand, the world-wide economic depression at the end of the decade led to difficulties in Finland too: bankruptcies, auctions of property and shortages. The language disputes, which had flared up once again, were a prominent issue throughout the 1920's and 1930's, but they did not lead to any legislation of note.

The great depression, which began at the end of the 1920's and continued until the middle of the next decade, was felt in Finland too, both financially and politically. Unemployment grew and in an agrarian country the fact that on a large scale smallholdings had such debts that they were forced to compulsory auctions was a disturbing phenomenon. Many banks were obliged to stop functioning or to merge with larger banks.

The social crisis naturally increased political pressures. Linked to this was the worry concerning the spread of communism and the developments within the Soviet Union. The collectivization and the population transfers in the Soviet Union gave visible reason to fear changes. It was under such circumstances that the anti-communist Lapua movement was born and grew. The movement which gained wide support in 1930 at the time of the great peasants' march to Helsinki gradually became more radical culminating in an attempt at an armed rebellion in spring 1932. The movement was part of a general European trend against liberalism and the parliamentarism of the 1920's: in place of the monetary power, moral degeneration which they represented, more state control

---

The Finnish parliamentary form of government was given splendid expression in the Classical-style granite Parliament House completed in 1931 (architect J.S. Sirén). The president and the government are accommodated in palatial administration buildings from the period of the Grand-Dutchy of Finland.

and planning were sought particularly so that new attempts at the failed leftist revolutions after the world war could be prevented. Although there had been a left wing revolution in Finland in 1918, Finland preserved a parliamentary model throughout the 1932 situation and its after effects. This soon drew Finland closer to the other Nordic countries particularly since the Baltic countries and especially Germany were moving in the 1930's to a one-party system and dictatorial power.

After 1932 in Finland too there was a movement to long-term governments. At first the government was weak as far as parliamentary support was concerned and it leant above all on the President (P.E. Svinhufvud). It stabilized the situation both politically and financially and began to move the emphasis of foreign policy away from the League of Nations towards the security system of the Nordic countries. In 1937, with a change in Presidents, the so-called "red-green" coalition was formed, in which the Agrarian Party and the Social Democrats began a long period of co-operation. As far as internal politics were concerned it meant the rejection of the 1918 division, agreement over the language disputes of the 1920's and 1930's, and the beginning of a social security system; as far as foreign policy was concerned it meant co-operation with the

Swedish Social Democrat government and the rejection of the German alternative. The Foreign Ministers were Anglophiles, the government coalition resembled slightly the French example, and the general direction was towards the Nordic countries. Financial development and a rise in the standard of living also muffled the right wing, and the fascist-like IKL Party which was born out of the Lapua movement was reduced to a minor factor.

The general liberalizing tone of the thirties was expressed in the Anglosaxon tone of the newspapers and films, whereas the stimulus for the pictorial arts and architecture came mostly from France. In place of Neo-Classicism came the Functionalist style with its predominance in building production, metal furniture and the Artek form based on the use of Finnish materials. In the field of philosophy and the "world view" logical empirism and the new trends in psychology, particularly freudism, received wide attention; the general trend in cultural life changed from the narrowly nationalistic to a more open attitude to Europe, and in the field of the natural sciences the influence of the United States began to be felt at the end of the decade.

In this optimistic atmosphere the threat of a great war did not lead to any considerable development in defensive preparedness in spite of the reports of Marshal Mannerheim, who had become chairman of the Defence Council at the beginning of the decade. When, therefore, the Soviet Union as early as 1938 secretly and in 1939 publicly demanded negotiations and exchanges of territory, Finland did not for a long time believe that the demands would lead to war. The Soviet Union's attack in November 1939 was to Finland and the world to a great extent a surprise.

The Soviet Union had that classic security problem: the need to shift the defence of Leningrad and north-west Russia back to the mouth of the Gulf of Finland, since on Finland's and Estonia's independence it had been obliged to draw the line very close to Leningrad. Estonia and the other Baltic countries did provide the Soviet Union with bases in autumn 1939; Finland was prepared to discuss changes of territory on the Karelian Isthmus, but did not feel it was possible to negotiate about a base on the Hanko peninsula.

Also the situation that had come about when the Soviet Union and Germany had entered into an alliance and had made a secret division of interests was for Finland quite new. Germany did remain neutral during the Winter War, according to agreement. Neither did Finland's hopes to realize a Nordic Country defence plan come

A Finnish anti-aircraft gun in field position during the Winter War. The darkness and coldness of mid-winter also had a psychological effect on both the Finns and even more so on the Russians.

During the Winter War the other frontiers of the world were quiet, and the attention of the whole world was directed at Finland which fought tenaciously under difficult conditions.

about: the country was obliged to go to war alone and ill-equipped.

But the Soviets too had difficulties and inexperience particularly in respect of winter warfare, and the Finnish army — whose Commander in Chief had become Marshal Mannerheim — achieved several considerable victories in repelling attacks. It was, however, clear that Finland could not last long against an enemy of far greater power. When the Soviet Union gave up its support to the marionette government it had established on the Karelian Isthmus, an armistice was concluded in March 1940. The Finnish army had withdrawn and was forced to surrender Viipuri (Vyborg) but the front held out until the end and partly guaranteed the preconditions for an honourable but heavy defeat. It realized the Soviet Union's original aims: a base in Hanko and the moving of the border further from Leningrad.

The area surrendered was about one tenth of Finland's area and the population slightly more: all Karelians thought it better to come to what was left of Finland than to remain in their home districts. In terms of those fallen and wounded Finland's losses in the Winter War had had been great. The Winter War left the Finns with a feeling of injustice which was mitigated by the awareness that the result, the maintenance of sovereignty, was gained by unanimity and resolution. These factors had an important effect in reorientation when relationships between the Soviet Union an Germany began to be strained. Germany began to show an interest in Finland and this was received in post-war Finland with a sense of relief, in a situation in which Soviet politics were interpreted in wide circles to be still anti-Finland. When Hitler attacked the Soviet Union in the summer of 1941 there were already German troops in northern Finland which became a German military area and an extension of the German-controlled Norway. Finland did not, however, form an alliance with Germany and both the Finnish government and the Commander in Chief followed strategy which served the purposes of Finland alone during the war. Thus Finland did not actively participate in the siege of Leningrad nor did it break Leningrad's service line to the Arctic Ocean. Mannerheim understood that Finland and the Soviet Union or Russia would still be neighbours even after the war. Finland did, however, occupy part of Eastern Karelia on the other side of the border. There were plans to annex this area to Finland. This was the area that Finland had tried to obtain in 1919 — 1920 and in 1939 the Soviet Union had offered this area to Finland as an exchange of territory and also annexed it to

Mika Waltari's novel Sinuhe the Egyptian, published in 1945, reflected post-war relativism and existential pessimism and received world acclaim with translations into many languages. The youth of his own faculty at the university erected a monument in his honour. It was completed in 1985 and was sculpted by Veikko Hirvimäki.

Finland with an agreement made that year
by the marionette governmet. Essentially,
however, it was a question of moving the
war into the adversary's territory, of a
tactical viewpoint and a potential territory
for exchange during the making of peace.

From the year 1943 onwards Finland
investigated the possibility of a separate
peace but on the one hand the situation
concerning supplies and the fear of a
German occupation, and on the other the
harsh peace terms postponed the armistice
until September 1944. In the spring of 1944
there had been heavy bombing of Helsinki
and severe fighting on the Isthmus during
the summer. At this point Finland made a
pact with Germany, terminated after as little
as two months, when paving the way for a
peace treaty with the Soviet Union.
Commander in Chief Mannerheim was
elected President of Finland.

The 1944 truce which was ratified at the
Paris Peace Congress of 1947, returned the
bordes to the situation in 1940 in Karelia;
instead of Hanko the peninsula of Porkkala
was now rented to the Soviets for 50 years.
Finland had to expel the Germans from
Lappland which took several months and
caused great devastation. It also had to agree
to pay heavy war reparations and accept
certain restrictions concerning the size of its
army, etc. But the country retained its

After the wars, in the cemetaries of all Finnish churches memorials to those who had given their lives for their country were erected alongside the graves of the fallen. One of the first is the statue in Saarijärvi in Central Finland. In the background can be seen the large wooden church of the parish in the typical Empire style of the beginning of the 19th century. In Finland nearly all the fallen heroes were removed from the battlefields to their home parishes. The patriotism of these memorials is always unassuming and dignified.

sovereignty and the Control Committee set up by the allies left the country immediately after the Paris Peace Treaty. The payment of reparations in full in 1952 and the Soviet Union's relinguishment of the Porkkala base in 1955 removed the last restrictions to sovereignty.

The 1941–44 war is known in Finland as the "continuation war" because it was understood as an extension of the Winter War and as an attempt to compensate for losses suffered in that war. The history behind the Winter War explains why Finland participated in the war alongside Germany:

in the great power competition between Germany and the Soviet Union/Russia, Finland could not have chosen the side of the Soviet Union in 1941. It was obliged to choose one side or the other for reasons of supplies and in order to avoid a possible occupation like that of Norway and Denmark. But Finnish state leaders and military leaders stressed consistently and with success the special character of Finland and its independence in the war. In Finland there was only very marginal interest in the ideology of national socialism, and the Finnish government refused all ideological co-operation with Germany and, for example, rejected entirely any proposed measures against Finland's jews. These factors made it possible to withdraw from the war a year before Germany's collapse and to turn their weapons against their former brothers in arms. But of course the change in direction was psychologically demanding particularly since fears concerning the aims of the Soviet Union were deep; the authority of Marshal Mannerheim, the President-Commander in Chief, in accepting peace and beginning war against the Germans in Lappland was decisive.

Finland felt its situation poor, difficult and threatened, relative to the Soviet Union, which had become a great power and

Sweden, which had avoided the war and become wealthy during it, the Baltic countries, which had lost their independence and Germany, which had become an economic and political void. In the continuation war Finland's number of fallen was 65 000 and wounded 158 000, homes had to be found for over 423 000 Karelians (representing 11 % Finland's population), jobs had to be found for those returning from war and the war reparations, which placed Finnish production under extreme conditions, had to be paid. The demands of the victors, the Soviet Union and Great Britain, to condemn the war guilty, that is to say the political leaders during the war, had a great psychological effect on the country. The war trials led to the conviction of the wartime President Ryti, two former Prime Ministers and some other political leaders to prison sentences of different lengths, at most ten years. However, compared to other countries which had participated in the war, Finland suffered relatively lightly. Above all this was due to the fact that neither side had occupied Finland; Finland's defence during the summer of 1944 would have made the occupation of the country too costly for the Soviet Union. Neither did Germany have adequate power to bend Finland, which had changed sides, to its will. Popular humour soon found expression, now become a

War-time meant a great migration of population. The most important of these was the placement of the 400 000 refugees from Karelia first in 1940 and then in 1944. The majority of these were given new smallholdings in different parts of Finland. Humanitarian aid from Sweden was

considerable. One expression of this was the reception of thousands of Finnish children to within the realm of healthy food and secure circumstances. The picture shows children leaving for Sweden. Parents believed that the wars would be short but for some the separation grew to be years.

classic, for the result of the war: the Soviet Union won but Finland came second.

As a consequence of the war Finland went throught a fast and at the beginning difficult economic and social change, and it took a long time before the level of pre-war production and standard of living were reached and passed. Such was the situation in other countries that had gone to war, although in Finland as a neighbour of the well-off Sweden, this was soon forgotten. But the period of change took place organizationally without radical changes in the social system. Finland's constitution of 1919 remained in force, and the government leant the whole while on a parliament elected by free elections. The highest decision-making power represented long traditions: the President-Commander in Chief Mannerheim, the Prime Minister and future President J.K. Paasikivi (elected to office in 1946) and the post-war Foreign Minister Carl Enckell had all been in leading political positions during the coming of independence

Paavo Nurmi lights the Olympic flame to mark the start of the Helsinki Olympic Games of 1952. The holding of the Games in Finland was not only a mark of respect for the country's sporting tradition but also a sign of the stabilization of Finland's international position. Economically, too, the country was emerging from the years of shortage following the war and rationing could be gradually brought to an end.

The success of an ordinary country girl in the beauty competitions of the world brought joy and pride to everyday life in post-war Finland. The 1952 Miss Universe Armi Kuusela together with her mother.

and they all knew Russia well even thought they were not experts in communist ideology. Among the younger politicians Urho Kekkonen of the Agrarian Party and K.A. Fagerholm of the Social Democrats, both of whom had been Prime Ministers during the Paasikivi period, had both been members of parliament and ministers as early as the 1930's, Fagerholm even in the war cabinet. In addition to the Agrarian

Party and the Social Democrats, the People's Democrats led by the communists were in the government 1945 – 48. The communist participation in the government had a remarkable effect on the stabilizing of internal politis in the immediate post-war years. The changeover in power in Czechoslovakia in spring 1948 also led to a change of government in Finland. Paasikivi formed a Social Democratic minority government led by Fagerholm even though this did not please the Soviet Union. The People's Democrats returned to government only in the 60's. In its foreign policy Finland gave most importance to cementing good relations with the Soviet Union even though this led to many difficult situations as the Cold War deepened. Thus Finland refused Marshall aid because of the political ties which this implied, but Finland did receive considerable loans from the United States which significantly helped in stabilizing the economic situation in the country. The payment of war reparations were carried out precisely and on schedule even though it put the national economy and industry under great strain. On the other hand this forced the country to restructure its industry which soon began to pay off. The loans received from the United States and Sweden were mostly used to modernize industry and develop exports.

From the military policy viewpoint the Finnish position was restricted by the conditions contained in the truce of 1944 and the Paris Peace Treaty of 1947 concerning the Finnish defence forces and the number of its weapons, conditions which the allies later mitigated. As early as 1945 Marshal Mannerheim stressed to the Soviet Union that it was also within Soviet interests that Finland had efficient defence forces. This led to the 1948 Treaty of Friendship, Co-operation and Mutual Assistance with the Soviet Union in which Finland agreed to prevent any attack on the Soviet Union through Finnish territory. The treaty has worked as intended and has freed the Soviet Union from the classical worry over the security of Leningrad, but there has never been any need to put into operation the article concerning consultations on the threat of attack through Finnish territory. The treaty is therefore a kind of declaration in principle and while renewing the treaty there has been no need to change the wording. The Finnish aim to remain outside conflicts between the great powers is mentioned at the beginning of this treaty.

The stabilizing influence of Finland's Soviet relations has been felt in wider circles around the Baltic Sea and from at least the beginning of the 1960's all the western powers have continuously recognized the

The Chairman of the Allied Supervisory Commission
Colonel General Zhdanov greeting the Finnish President
J.K. Paasikivi. Both the Russian and the Finnish leaders, the
presidents Marshal Mannerheim and Paasikivi worked hard
to create correct and proper relations with the former enemy.

success of Finland's policy of neutrality. Even so, Finland, as a good but non-socialist neighbour of the Soviet Union, has received varying degrees of understanding in the western countries. When international tension has decreased it has been admired, during periods of tension between the great powers there have been doubts concerning Finnish independence and credibility − not on the part of governments but in some sectors of the foreign press. Thus it has remained un-noticed that the relationship between Finland and the Soviet Union is built upon the basic geographic-strategic factors of the Baltic Sea and the Gulf of Finland. Soviet security interests and Finland's desire not to become the arena for a conflict between the great powers − to avoid repeating the situation which led to the wars of 1939 and 1941 − are independent of everyday events. In a very real way these military and political viewpoints are supported by mutual economic interests.

Finland also initiated economic co-operation with the Soviet Union and from 1952 onwards a great share of the products of the war reparation industry became export articles to the Soviet Union.

The period which began in 1944 and particularly the period which started in 1952 after the payment of war reparations resembled the situation at the turn of the century. The Soviet Union's large markets and the Finnish structure of production fit each other well. About 15 to 25 % of Finnish exports have gone to the Soviet Union and for long periods Finland has been the Soviet Union's greatest non-socialist trading partner after West Germany: the Soviet Union has alternated first with England and then with Sweden as Finland's greatest partner. The main import from the Soviet Union has been energy; natural gas, nuclear power and above all oil, whereas Finland exports consumer goods such as clothes, shoes and furniture as well as machines and most visibly shipping, ice-breakers and large construction projects, in which the Finns have planned and built in the areas of Leningrad, Karelia and Estonia not only hospitals and hotels but also large harbours and entire industrial towns.

Entering into the great volume of Soviet trade and embarking on long term projects meant a great change in the structure of production immediately after the war. The war reparations demanded by the Soviet Union had to be paid in the form of products defined by the victor and this forced Finland to speed up its process of industrialization. Commerce between Finland and the Soviet Union has made the relationship between the two countries more practical and concrete. Trade has thus

The ice-breaker has become a matter of technical pride for Finland: concentration on the demanding but specialized technical know-how sector has helped preserve the profitability of Finland's ship-building industry at a time when ship-building in other countries has had to rely on massive subventions.

removed prejudices and those psychological constraints which were brought about by the experiences of war, by the difference in language and culture, and by the differences between socialist societies and market economy democracies. In addition there is still the difference in size between a world power and a small state — in Leningrad alone there are about the same amount of people as in the whole of Finland. It has been of mutual interest to both countries to show that peaceful coexistence between countries of different social systems can function well. Finnish foreign policy led to the fact that at the end of the sixties and during the seventies Helsinki was accepted as neutral territory for important international negotiations in addition to the classical Vienna and Geneva.

Another cornerstone of Finnish post-war politics was the strengthening of co-operation with the other Nordic countries and particularly with Sweden. Especially after the Baltic countries had been annexed to the Soviet Union and after the economic and cultural impact of Germany in the area of the Baltic Sea had weakened, the Nordic countries — Finland, Sweden, Norway, Denmark and Iceland — drew even closer together. This was expressed by the formation of the Nordic Council, which is an inter-parliamentary body, and many other

Vice President

organs for co-operation particularly in the fields of culture and administration.

The 1960's meant closer economic ties between Finland and Sweden as the movements of the labour force and capital grew quickly, as did trade between the two countries. Finland and Sweden are bound together by innumerable individual and family relationships, cultural ties and a number of joint associations, youth organizations and enterprises. Swedish is still the second national language in Finland and, from the 1960's onwards, every Finnish child has had to learn its basics at school. After the migration from Finland to Sweden in the 1960's Finnish has had a more prominent position in Sweden. Air traffic and particularly boat traffic between Stockholm and Helsinki and Turku and over the Gulf of Bothnia has increased and thousands of people and dozens or hundreds of lorries are carried over every day.

The close relationship between Finland and Sweden as well as between Finland and the other Nordic countries is also expressed in the co-operation between the main political parties, the Social Democrats and Centre Parties. This co-operation reflects the similarity of the Nordic societies and, at the same time, strengthtens their cohesion.

Despite the differences, development has gone towards the so-called Welfare State in

Left: Intercourse between the Nordic countries also takes place at the party level. In the picture are Finland's and Sweden's Social Democrat prime ministers Kalevi Sorsa (right) and Olof Palme at the International Social Democrat Organization's disarmament conference in Vienna in 1985.

Overleaf: Large — from the point of view of the landscape too large — and very handsome and modern car ferries. The traffic between Finland and Sweden is enormous. The business world uses these ships as places to hold meetings and seminars and a journey by ship has become a great source of entertainment; shopping, museum or theatre trips between the two neighbouring countries are frequent.

the creation of which the wealthy Sweden, having been spared the war, had a start over the other Nordic countries and in part also acted as an example. The national solidarity in Finland is, however, partly based on other values, particularly on the efforts during and after the war, so that the general trend in Finnish development has been slower and more conservative than that of Sweden. Correspondingly its construction has been based on greater internal unity, which has been expressed at the political level by continuous coalition governments.

The fast urbanization and industrialization of the country during the 1950's created internal tensions not without foreign policy implications, which were brought to the fore in the 1956 Presidential election. In the electoral college Kekkonen, the candidate for the Agrarian Party won by the smallest possible majority (151 − 149) over the Social Democrat Fagerholm. In the final stage of the election the former received the support of the People's Democrats and the latter of the Conservatives and Liberals. From the point of view of foreign policy Kekkonen was considered a symbol of the Paasikivi doctrine, whereas Fagerholm was considered the representative of the Nordic-western doctrine even though the differences in fact were hardly very great. During Kekkonen's first term of office, first in 1958 with

Fagerholm as Prime Minister and later in 1961, Soviet concern over the reflection of great power politics was expressed twice but both times doubts were overcome.

Finland was in fact the only country involved in the second world war which completely fulfilled its obligations to repay the war debt. War reparations had to be paid in the form of industrial goods and this led to a great extent to a change in Finnish industryl production structure and the renewal of machinery. The importance of the metal industry in particular grew greatly and it developed from a home market industry to an export industry. The traditional export industry, wood processing, expanded and

Along with fast industrialization the participation of women in working life increased rapidly and made child care a central issue in Finland too. Differing political views have, however, reached a rather large degree of unanimity concerning the support of different forms of child care. Both municipal and private day-care centres receive support.

was modernized rapidly and exports to western countries began soon after the war. In 1961, in order to secure the preconditions of its most important industry, Finland joined EFTA, the European Free Trade Association, and later in 1973 made an extensive customs agreement with the European Economic Community. On both occasions the country was able to secure its economic interests and still emphasize its independence of the political ties of these

---

Finnish design achieved considerable international success in the 1950's. It was based on the elegant and unassuming use of basic materials and on a classical simplicity. Tapio Wirkkala's "shell" is a ply-wood sculpture from 1956.

Finnish design from 1980: a velvet suit designed by Vuokko Nurmesniemi.

economic organizations. The agreement with the EEC was followed by a customs agreement with the East European COMECON. The post-war economic growth which continued until 1974 also fully benefited Finland, even though the first post-war years was a period of heavy investment and war reparations. The renovation of industry was followed, from the 1950's

onwards, by significant construction work. The modern road network, electrification, a dense network of internal air traffic and the construction of dwellings particularly in towns was carried out very quickly in the sparsely populated and large country. This was followed by the rapid development of different forms of social security, the system of schools and higher education in the

Fast urbanization demands a great deal of community planners and architects. The picture shows the suburb of Tapiola to the west of Helsinki. Care has been taken to preserve the elements of forest and the sea.

1960's. All these both increased the general level of welfare as well as reduced social differences and differences between areas.

While Finland in the 1930's was still a very agrarian country, its great period of urbanization and industrialization was late compared to that of many other countries and was correspondingly rather fast. This was naturally reflected in political life as well as in the development of attitudes and ideologies. The housing and placing in productive life of the Karelians and those returning from the front was to be confronted immediately after the war. As the

towns and industry could not yet employ all this group, a great number of them were settled in smallholdings but these proved to be of little worth and played their part in the new great period of migration in the 1960's. Despite the efforts of the Agrarian and People's Democratic Parties in particular to improve the standard of living in the poor areas of eastern and northern Finland life could not be improved there without great

Outdoor activities and skiing gather Finns together to enjoy their weekends. For example in the surroundings of Helsinki are large municipal hiking and skiing forests.

agricultural subsidies. When, after the 1966
election, the Social Democrats became the
leading government party the rationalization
of agriculture was carried out. This meant
putting an end to particularly unprofitable
smallholdings in northern Finland. The
consequence was great migration to the
towns of southern Finland and to Sweden
whose expanding industry at that time
needed a great deal of manpower.
Understandably this "great migration"
caused a lot of social problems and was also

The summer cottage is a central part of the Finnish way of life. Their construction quickly became common in the 1950's and 1960's as a counterbalance to urbanization and because of fast travelling by car. Little by little, however, the use of the summer cottage has decreased because of foreign travel and the various summer cultural events as well as "new" forms of sport such as sailing and tennis.

refelected very noticably in Finnish literature. The vigorous and popular literary genre of novels and epic literature concentrated for a long time on describing the mental impact of this period of change.

The competition between towns and rural areas, consumers and producers, industry and agriculture has governed Finnish post-war politics — a fact that has not been without foreign policy implications either. As real as competition, however, has been the fact that the leading parties, the Social Democrats and the Agrarians have together formed a coalition government for most of the post-war period, never on their own it is true, but always as if softened by the inclusion of smaller parties. The authority and often concrete political leadership of the President of the Republic has been a very real part of the politics of compromise within the government, as has the constitutional statutory majority regulations which demand a 2/3 or even 5/6 majority in parliament for the most important bills. The coalitions have been different at the level of local politics. The Conservative Party has, with the exception of two short periods, been an opposition party at the national level but has at the local level and particularly in larger towns been a dominant party and often in coalition with the Social Democrats.

After the first post-war (1945) election the People's Democrats, which gained a great popularity, took part in government together with the Agrarians and Social Democrats. This was of great significance during the period of major changes; the participation of the People's Democrats in the government brought many advantages to the workers but at the same time prevented extensive strikes and demonstrations. In 1948, after the events in Czechoslovakia, President Paasikivi nominated a Social Democrat minority government led by Fagerholm. This government lasted for about two years despite the suspicions of the Soviet Union and was followed by a number of coalition governments led by Urho Kekkonen as Prime Minister in which the Agrarians were the leading party. When, in 1956, Kekkonen became President he, in turn, nominated his competitor Fagerholm as Prime Minister, but this government came up against internal difficulties, mainly caused by the Soviet Union's suspicions during the stifling Cold War. After the Soviet Union had stopped trade and having called their Ambassador home, the coalition government broke up and the Social Democratic Party split into two for a long time. Only after the 1966 election did the re-united Social Democrats become the leading government party and in addition to the Agrarians the People's Democrats too were in the government. This reflected President Kekkonen's striving for national unification which, during the period of social changes, was as important as immediately after the war. The Communists,

During his 25-year term of office, President Kekkonen successfully kept different elements together thanks to his dynamic and many-sided personality. Far left: Among gold-washers in Lapland. Next to this, receiving Prime Minister A. Kosygin off the Moscow train. Below, giving his annual New Year speech to the people and above, speaking to the sculptress Laila Pullinen: he was very close to art and intellectual circles.

however, did not remain in the government for long and during the 1970's their periods in the government compared to the Social Democrats and Agrarians were short. At the beginning of the 1980's support for the Communist Party declined rapidly.

At the end of the 1960's a new protest party came into being alongside the People's Democrats. The smallholders' or Rural Party (Vennamo), representing the outlying districts of eastern Finland, even became a government party in the 1980's. The longest-standing small party in the government has been the Swedish Party, but the Liberal Party, which was often a government party in the 1950's and 1960's, was faced with a crisis in the 1970's and withered away during the 1980's. The opposition has generally comprised the People's Democrats-Communists on the one hand and the Conservative Party, which gained in popularity during the 1970's, on the other. The Finnish government has thus been one of the centre-left with the balance changing at times.

The advantage of the coalition governments has been the securing of large

---

Waves of both hippies and revolutionaries arrived in Finland too in the 1960's as an expression of a new youth culture: the general message was peace and love as the banner shows.

representation of different groups in society. On the other hand, this has often resulted in compromises and costly situations. At one time this could be seen in rapid inflation, loud political quarrelling and a concentration on personalities. Government by coalition, in the post-oil crisis period, became under the leaderhsip of President Kekkonen government by consensus. Society had become stabilized after the great migration and youth unrest, and under the external pressure by the price-development of industry, Finland moved into a period of successful economic policy whose aim was, by supporting industry and its competativeness, to maintian employment and economic growth. Thus the

---

Designed by Alvar Aalto, Finlandia Hall on the banks of the bay of Töölö in Helsinki with Parliament House and the National Museum in the background. The grand concert and congress palace was built at the end of the 1960's although the spirit of the time was against monumental constructions, but the aim was to make

modernization of production carried out in Finland largely under the leadership of the left was completed earlier and more succesfully than in most European countries and based on a broad mutual national understanding.

The positive economic development from the end of the 1970's for at least ten years onwards has also had great significance as far as the external esteem of the country is concerned. Finland's policy of neutrality and its position in the world has not always been easily understood abroad. Extensive and succesful state visits by President Kekkonen made Finland's position and aims widely known, at the same time extensive cultural and economic co-operation with other

Helsinki a place of international conferences. This aim, which is part of Finland's objective to make its neutral and independent position generally recognized, was given grand expression in 1975 when the 'Helsinki Agreement' was signed in Finlandia Hall.

Finland is well known as a country of books and literature, with a vigorous institution of libraries, publishing companies and book shops. The Academic Book Store in Helsinki is known for its scientific and foreign sections and the splendid shop itself designed by Alvar Aalto.

countries brought a lot of visitors to Finland to see the country and its circumstances with their own eyes. Kekkonen was able to see the result of his work when Finland received as guests the heads of state and heads of government of 35 countries who signed the Helsinki agreement in Helsinki in 1975 at the final stage of the European Conference on Security and Co-operation in Europe. This made the Finnish capital and Finland's political aims more widely known in the world.

In Finland as elsewhere the post-war great age groups went to school in the 1950's and to universities and other institutes of higher education at the end of the 1960's. The ideological and moral change of the age was strongly felt as was the above-mentioned wave of urbanization which took place at the same time. In university politics a great decentralization programme had already been initiated which was far-reaching in Finland and was followed by strict *numerusclausus*-policy; Sorsa's period of consensus has

The central position of the President of the Republic in the Finnish constitution has made official state visits an important feature of Finnish foreign policy during the times of the Presidents Kekkonen and Koivisto. The picture shows the President of the Federal Republic of Germany, baron and Mrs R. von Weizsäcker as guests of President and Mrs Koivisto. Like queens the wives of Presidents have been the recipients of Grand Crosses since the 1980's.

corresponded to — perhaps too — peaceful academic and cultural life in which society has favoured above all "useful" and applied teaching and research. Demands have been made, however, on behalf of move ideological debate and criticism and during the 1980's Finnish cultural life has once again begun to orientate itself towards its roots in classical Europe.

Presidenti Kekkonen was re-elected to office in 1962, in 1968, in 1974 and in 1978.